The Designs of
KATHIE WINKLE
for James Broadhurst & Sons Ltd 1958-1978

by Peter Leath

Introduction by Maureen Batkin

Kathie Winkle, 1962

CONTENTS

ACKNOWLEDGEMENTS

I wish to extend my warmest thanks to Kathie Winkle for her generous help and support. During the collecting, the research and the cataloguing for this book I had cause to be grateful to many people who have loaned precious pieces for photography, others who have given their valuable time, and dealers who have helped us in our collecting.

My thanks to: Bob and Joan Anderson, David Back, Maureen Batkin, Lynn and Tony Blake, James and Margot Bonsfield, Les Davis, Graham Ford, Rodney Hampson, Viv and John Hicks, Lorraine Jacobs, Steve Jenkins, Carol Moore, Eddie Orme, Mrs Pamela Payne, Denny and Dazzle Parker, Peter Rimmer, Mel Robins, Andrew, Michael and Stephen Roper and the staff of Churchill China, Gianmarco Segato of Canada, stallholders and staff of Kingston Antiques Market, Ceramics Department of the Stoke-on-Trent City Museum and Arts Gallery, *The Sentinel* newspaper, Mr and Mrs Terry Thompson, Ian and Jane Watson, Ron and Carol Miller, Adam Wright. Special thanks to my wife, Sally.

PL

Thanks are due to Rodney Hampson for his help and encouragement and for the generous way he has allowed me to quote freely from his own researches. Many others have helped in a number of ways: Kathie Winkle, Michael and Stephen Roper and Reg Chilton who have given their time for interviews. They have patiently answered questions and allowed me to delve into factory records and archive material. I am grateful to them and to Malkin Ltd., and K.H. Bailey & Son for the loan of photographs, technical advice on rubber-stamping and for giving me the opportunity to photograph stamping equipment and pages from order books.

Special thanks must go to Peter Leath who has compiled this book, his wife, Sally, and other avid collectors who have relentlessly scoured the country, tracking down the examples of Kathie Winkle's rubber stamp designs, thus bringing into focus the scope and variety of her work for Broadhurst.

MB

Photography by Magnus Dennis
Edited by Sue Evans
Reproduction by Flaydemouse, Yeovil, Somerset, England
Published by Richard Dennis, The Old Chapel, Shepton Beauchamp, Somerset TA19 OLE, England
© 1999 Richard Dennis, Peter Leath & Maureen Batkin
ISBN 0 903685 67 1
All rights reserved
British Library Cataloguing-in-Publication Data. A catalogue record for this book is available from the British Library.

JAMES BROADHURST AND SONS
BY MAUREEN BATKIN

This book shows the results of a remarkable coincidence of events: a modernised tableware factory, a young and thrusting management who, when the demand came for her style of patterns, found their designer already in-house. The 113 designs illustrated here are the best witness to the design ability of Kathie Winkle, backed by the Roper family and the staff at James Broadhurst & Sons, Portland Works, Fenton, Stoke-on-Trent, between 1958 and 1978.

James Broadhurst & Sons' warehouse completed in May 1974.

The history of James Broadhurst & Sons can be traced back more than one hundred and fifty years. It had its beginnings with James Broadhurst I who, having been in partnerships since 1847, made the decision to become his own master. In 1854 he established a business making earthenwares at the Crown Works, Longton, and within two years he had been joined by his sons. It was at this time, 1856, that the name of James Broadhurst & Sons was established. Although the name is not as well-known as the likes of Minton, Wedgwood and Spode, Broadhurst, as with other family-run businesses, was the backbone of the Staffordshire pottery industry. The name was retained until 1984 when Churchill was adopted as an easily recognisable name for the entire group.

Rodney Hampson in his pioneering work, *Churchill China, Great British Potters Since 1795*, provides detailed histories of Broadhurst and all the companies within the group, set against a background of socio-economic changes. Therefore, no attempt has been made to cover this ground except when events have a direct bearing on the story of Kathie Winkle, as it is her work for the company which is being appraised.

Our story begins in 1941 when Broadhurst suffered a double blow with the death of Mr Edward Roper and when, as part of the Government Concentration Scheme, production ceased at the Portland Works, Victoria Road, Fenton, which the firm had occupied since 1870. His son, Peter Roper, joined the R.A.F. and the modest amount of ware needed to cater for their existing home trade customers was supplied by W.H. Grindley & Co. Naturally, after the cessation of hostilities, Broadhurst's was anxious to get back to normal production as soon as possible. Peter Roper reopened the works in 1945 and the making of earthenware was resumed but, like many other firms, Broadhurst was frustrated by the fact that, despite enormous demand, home supply was strictly limited by the government in order to earn the country much needed foreign currency. In the event, the restriction whereby undecorated ware and decorated seconds only were available for the home market, remained in place until 1952.

Peter Roper, Chairman from 1959-1984.

During the war years and into the early 1950s, domestic wares were made in circumstances where cheapness, utility and durability counted for more than ornament. In this sense, the International Style 'functionalism' played its part. In the post-war reconstruction period there was a definite rejection of functionalism as an aesthetic and as an ideal, although the functional tradition was, by that time, recognised as having vernacular roots within industry. Design reformers were given a second chance and, this time, industrial design was seen as a way forward, a way to shape the future in terms of social equality, with beauty being available to all and decoration and colour the order of the day. Broadhurst's policy was quite clear, theirs was an

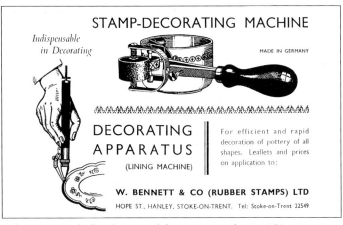

Advertisement for hand-operated decorating machine, 1950s.

industrial pottery making wares for the mass market and not made to display in cabinets.

Kathie Winkle joined the firm in 1950, just two years before wartime restrictions were lifted. At that time, the decorating department was in the capable hands of Mr Wilfred Morgan, decorating manager since 1947. Before the war he had worked for Doulton, Woods and Susie Cooper. When Kathie started at Broadhurst, a few semi-automatic making machines had been installed but everything was driven by the single steam engine. Most of the decoration then was underglaze painting and lining, although some rubber-stamping by hand was also being done, since transfer-printing had not been resumed. There were about six people hand-stamping and between twenty and thirty paintresses out of a total workforce of about seventy. (Decorators worked hard and could earn as much as £5 per week, good money at that time.)

It is hard to imagine the feeling of optimism in the late-1940s and early post-Festival of Britain years, but this was a period of economic rebirth with manufactured goods playing a major role. Peter Roper, Broadhurst's new managing director, was at the centre of the new movement. He had the foresight to invest much of the profit of the post-war boom in re-equipping and modernising the works with the aim to increase output and sales by modern mass-production methods. By the mid-1950s, Broadhurst began to formulate their large-scale modernisation plan to increase production by one-third. This involved demolition of the existing bottle biscuit and glost ovens and installing continuous kilns which were fully operational in 1956.

According to Reg Chilton, when he joined the firm as decorating manager in 1954, all the designs were hand-stamped, simple repeat patterns using stamps of 2ins x 1in or 3ins x 2ins, which were quick and easy to use. After

modernisation, output rose to about 16,000 dozen pieces a week although, not surprisingly, the emphasis was still on cost-effective underglaze decoration such as rubber-stamping, which was not only inexpensive but was also extremely versatile. Nor was there any problem in recruiting decorators. *The Pottery Gazette* recorded that The Stoke-on-Trent Youth Employment Service reported in December 1955, that in the fourteen months ended September 1954, no less than 942 girls and 629 boys commenced employment in the North Staffordshire pottery industry. Young girls could be trained in this simple form of handwork in a very short time and decorating absorbed 609 of the girls. In addition to underglaze decorating, the firm gradually introduced more onglaze decoration with first one and later three gilding machines. Technically, this placed Broadhurst's in a fairly strong position but, like other producers, they became increasingly aware of the need for new and innovative designs.

Reg Chilton, decorating manager, 1992.

Interestingly, a new generation of industrial designers was beginning to have an impact in the ceramic industry, as elsewhere. The Royal College of Art in London had been drawn into the great design debate. Founded in 1837, it was originally a school of design with the essential purpose of training students in the application of the arts to manufacture. Over the years, under various principals including Sir Edward Poynter and Sir William Rothenstein, the College seemed to have lost direction. A turning point came in the mid-1930s when it began to return to its original purpose. The movement was particularly marked

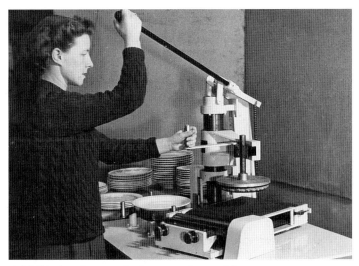

A Malkin hand-operated, plate-stamping machine.

after the war and could be seen in the School of Ceramics under Professor R.W. Baker.

In *The Pottery Gazette* review of the College end-of-year exhibition of 1953, it was pointed out that the main purpose in training students at this time was to lead them straight into the industry 'in its task of satisfying the pottery needs of the millions.' As evidence of this purpose they exhibited the designs of past students who, they stated, were gainfully employed with prominent pottery firms. These included Peter Wall for Wedgwood; Peter Cave and Hazel Thumpston for E. Brain; Tom Arnold for Ridgway and Adderley; and Doreen Penfold for Wattisfield Potteries.

As far as design-style was concerned, the editor of the *Decorative Art Year Book* for 1955/56 was undoubtedly in touch with the new developments in ceramic designs when he came to his conclusion that, 'Contemporary design for the home and its furnishings is winning popular acceptance and is here to stay.' Nevertheless, it should be noted that until that time most Staffordshire manufacturers tried to convince themselves that new trends in ceramics on the continent and in America had only a limited appeal and therefore no commercial basis. Midwinter was among the first to produce wares in the contemporary style but soon other Staffordshire potteries including Ridgway, Burgess & Leigh, and John Beswick were to introduce their own experimental designs.

Broadhurst's answer was to take on Margaret Turner, a young art school-trained local designer. She worked for the firm for approximately two years starting in about 1956 and may have been responsible for a number of figurative designs such as *Matador*, *Shanghai* and similar designs of that period. Additionally, *Alton*, *Star*, *Bouquet* and *Hawaii*, brought out in

1957 and *Revel* in 1958, could be by the same designer. Other possible designs by Margaret Turner are *Wheat Rose*, *Fiji* and *Tahiti* from the Island Ware series, but in the absence of further information at this time, it is is impossible to assess her full contribution. Kathie Winkle was, however, one of the other designers for the above series namely *Lyndhurst* and *Horizon*, and she recalls drawing up bits for the *Madeira* and *Tobago* patterns as well as the backstamp.

KATHIE WINKLE DESIGNS

Kathie Winkle, born in 1932, was a local girl. She started her working life as a painter for Shorter & Son at the age of fifteen, leaving two-and-a-half years later, in 1950, to join the more progressive firm of Broadhurst as a piecework paintress. That same year, Broadhurst acquired their first Ryckman gold-edge lining machine from Malkin, making them one of the first to install such a machine – eventually they had three. In common with other family-run businesses, there was a rapport between master and worker and Kathie, after several years of piecework painting, was encouraged to try her hand at designing. However, it was some time before her creative talent became apparent and her artistic influence came into play, making her debut with *Pedro*, introduced by Broadhurst in 1958. Early designs, including *Pedro*, were unsigned when they first went into production but were usually marked later if they continued to be successful.

Michael and Stephen Roper in the factory showroom.

Kathie Winkle's success in the design field coincided with the rise of the baby-boom generation which nurtured a throwaway economy where design obsolescence was accepted and 'Fitness for Need' rather than 'Fitness for Purpose' became the order of the day. Broadhurst was aware of the gap in the market for cheap and cheerful ranges which could be filled with their own production lines and made a good choice when they singled out the young and enthusiastic Kathie to fill that gap. She was an intuitive designer with a good eye for pattern and was familiar with contemporary trends. More importantly, she had a sound knowledge of the making and design processes which only come from working directly with the ware. Even William Morris would have approved! Kathie says she had no formal training although, when she describes her work as being more 'technical than artistic', she underestimates her contribution to the design process. The fact that her designs were successful over a long period is an indication of her talent. Designing on such a large commercial scale was even more remarkable, considering her modest artistic background. Kathie Winkle's designs for Broadhurst are evidence that she was equally at home designing floral patterns such as *Autumn* or *San Tropez* as she was creating her well-known abstract, geometric repetitive designs like *Eclipse* and *Michelle*. The simple colour renderings of her designs, especially the browns, greens, oranges and yellows reminiscent of Midwinter, capture the essence of Sixties' and Seventies' design but, above all, Kathie Winkle's unpretentious designs are pure fun.

Designing for Broadhurst seems to have been very much an ad hoc affair as there was no designated design department. Kathie tells me that she either worked to order

Malkin hollow-ware stamping machine.

when a customer asked the firm's representative for something specific, or she might be asked by a member of the Roper family to produce a range of patterns. At first Peter Roper himself had an input both in the design process and in selecting the designs for production. Later influences came from his sons, Michael and Stephen. Inspiration for new designs was gained from various sources, contemporary trends in ceramics, wallpapers and textiles and, due to the contemporary nature of most patterns, designs were frequently changed – unless, of course, they proved to be particularly popular.

By the 1960s Broadhurst had successfully increased production with about 80% of their sales for the home market. As part of a new sales drive to capture the growing markets, Broadhurst initiated selling direct to supermarkets and chain stores in presentation packs and, responding to the catalogue culture, pioneered boxed sets to attract the highly competitive mail order business as well as boosting their export sales. Littlewoods, Great Universal Stores and Grattan were among their mail order clients. These firms brought out new catalogues at regular intervals and their customers expected a choice of eye-catching designs, which Broadhurst's and Kathie were able to provide. Catalogue trade was an important outlet because here it was possible to sell ware in slightly higher price ranges, on easy payment plans.

Although there was little need for catalogue companies to attribute wares, during the design-conscious Fifties and Sixties, named designers became an excellent selling ploy for other outlets. Taking the lead in this direction were trendy companies such as Midwinter who, influenced by the Scandinavian attitude to design, began to acknowledge designers even to the point of incorporating the designer's name in the company backstamp. Had Broadhurst not had a Kathie Winkle, they would have needed to invent one.

In an export drive, Stephen Roper visited Australia in 1964 and took with him four new geometric patterns showing Kathie Winkle's influence which were very well received. These simple repeat pattern designs were in vogue and very much the type of decoration at which Broadhurst and Kathie Winkle would excel. Michael Roper, director and technical manager, made a sales trip to Canada in 1964 and it was mainly in response to a request from a Canadian customer that the 'A Kathie Winkle Design' backstamp was created. This ensured that Kathie's name was as well-known abroad as at home. She had a natural affinity to designing for the stamping process and some of her best designs stem from this period.

Hand-stamping had long been a speciality of the firm.

Underglaze decorating department.

This unsophisticated form of decorating had its roots in the nineteenth-century cut-sponge printing technique and was developed during this century with the wider use of India rubber. The most common use within the ceramic industry was for company backstamps, lettering and for simple designs. Suppliers to the industry such as Wengers included India rubber stamps in their catalogues and, in addition to open stock stamps which were sold to anyone, special designs could also be made to order. These were more expensive in the first instance because of the cost of making the pattern which could be wood, soft metal or brass, but, as might be expected, subsequent orders would cost very little. Most of the stamps used by Broadhurst were made by W. Bennett (Rubber Stamps) Ltd., a local company which set up in Hanley in the early 1920s.

From the early 1950s, hand-stamping was supplemented by Malkin's stamping machine, first designed for gold printing and developed for underglaze printing by Broadhurst and Bilton. The early stamping machines were quite basic and the technique, although fast in a good operator's hands, had a restricted colour palette and poor definition. Also, while it was relatively easy to stamp onto flat surfaces, stamping other shapes proved to be difficult and it is possible to find sets with printed plate and saucer centres while the cups, jugs and bowls were decorated with coloured slip or aerographed.

All Kathie Winkle's designs from the later 1950s were printed onto the ware by semi-automatic rubber-stamping machines supplied by Malkin. The stamps were made by Bennett's to Kathie's own drawings. Once the design was accepted, she would redraw this to scale in black ink on white card for Bennett's. This, in itself, was a highly-skilled job when considering the range and shapes of items produced. Finally, Bennett's would make the engravings, from which they would make moulds for the rubber stamps. Designs could also be, and were, purchased directly from the rubber stamp supplier although these would also be adapted for production by Kathie and others, working closely with the rubber stamp company. Rejected designs were not wasted but might be cut and up and incorporated into new patterns.

As a form of pottery decoration, rubber-stamping reached its zenith in the Sixties and early Seventies through Kathie Winkle's work for Broadhurst. The black outlines were applied to the unglazed body with simple rubber stamps and then filled in with hand-painted colours as appropriate, before glazing. The beauty of this 'stamp and fill' process was that colouring could be reduced to a bare minimum. Time and motion was carefully calculated for each new pattern, every brushstroke counted, and paintresses worked with a limited palette, usually three colours or less. Decorators were given the choice of working individually on each piece, or in groups each painting in one colour, if it was a multicolour design. An experienced

Malkin bowl-stamping machines.

7

A decorator completing the 50,000,000th piece of *Rushstone*, 1975.

decorator would probably produce in the region of 100 dozen pieces a day. One of Broadhurst's most successful designs, *Rushstone*, was produced in this period. This was one of a number of designs created in collaboration with Reg Chilton, the decorating manager, who in this instance had the original idea, and Kathie, using her skill as a designer, was able to adapt this for production. The firm recorded that *Rushstone* passed the 50 million mark in 1975 and eventually exceeded 100 million pieces.

EXPANSION AND AUTOMATION

In 1965 Broadhurst was in a strong market position at home and abroad. They completed a successful show at the trade fair with their boxed ware which included some with matching cutlery and table-linen, their 88-piece Home maker sets also included glassware. *Kofti* pots for serving both tea and coffee, were also offered and there were 23-piece *Kofti* sets made for the South African market. Time was ripe for expansion when Broadhurst made the decision to acquire all the ordinary shares in the old-established firm of Sampson Bridgwood. Peter, Michael and Stephen Roper were appointed new directors. Bridgwood brought with it a site over three times the size of the Portland Pottery and an old factory with some post-war modernisation, the extra capacity Broadhurst so badly needed. The Bridgwood factory was making mostly hotel ware, an area of production

they wished to expand, and some earthenware. According to Reg Chilton, 'They had a couple of chaps who were designers but designs came from a number of sources, including some from newly-qualified design students who went around factories selling their work.' Some Broadhurst rubber stamp designs were produced at Bridgwood's alongside their hotel ware.

With the expansion came increased mechanisation. Throughout the 1970s, F. Malkin & Co., manufacturers of ceramic-decorating machinery, developed many new techniques for decorating tableware, identifying the need and fulfilling that need with equipment designed specifically for a certain job, be it rubber-stamping in colour or gold, lining and banding, spray-glazing, screen-printing etc. The production of *bisque* (fired but unglazed pottery) became largely automated and in 1974 Broadhurst achieved their highest output for a decade, producing over one million dozen pieces a year. This was achieved because the firm had installed three automatic ginnetting (glostware cleaning) machines, two new automatic plate-making machines and four Dekram printing machines which transferred prints from engravings, by a silicone pad, to the ware. A new 25,000 square feet building for automatic making, a biscuit kiln and underglaze decorating, had been erected.

Dekram machines were used for printing *Constable* designs, reproductions of the famous artist's work, issued to coincide

Kiln drawers.

with the 200th anniversary of his birth in 1774. Castle prints, designed by Roy Durber, were also issued using Dekram machines, with a series to suit individual countries, Danish Castles and Austrian Schlosses amongst them. After 1975, few new Kathie Winkle designs were produced, although order books show that many old favourites such as *Viscount*, *Calypso* and others, were still available through mail order company catalogues and for the export markets.

Over the next few years significant changes were taking place. Many of the earlier machine-decorating techniques had been combined, resulting in one person producing multicolour screen-printed and banded ware at a rate of sixteen pieces per minute. Without any intermediate handling or drying process, *bisque* ware was supplied directly from stock, decorated, and off-loaded directly on to a Malkin automatic spraying line, and from the glazing line directly into cranks, ready for placing and firing. ('Cranks' are the supports which separate the pieces during the second glost firing.) Utilising this system of combined decorating, auto-glazing and direct cranking, losses due to intermediate handling between processes of screen-printing banding and glazing were reduced to a minimum, storage space between processes eliminated and direct labour content reduced by 50%. By 1978, this system could produce on a daily basis 24,000 decorated and glazed pieces in an eight-hour working day with a direct labour involvement of seven people.

A year later this modular system was extended to include multicolour silicone pad printing, a system which had been used in the plastic industry for a number of years but only recently adopted by the ceramic industry. These machines offered greater scope and flexibility and top-of-the-range models could produce eight-colour pad prints at up to fifteen pieces per minute or four-colour decorations at a speed of twenty-five to thirty pieces per minute. Mechanisation overtook most methods of hand-decoration in this period and, sadly, marked the end of the road for Kathie Winkle and her band of decorators at Broadhurst. In 1978 she changed roles and became a quality-control manageress until her retirement in 1992, bringing to a close a small, but nevertheless important, chapter in the history of ceramic design and decoration.

BIBLIOGRAPHY
Hampson, Rodney *Churchill China: Great British Potters Since 1795*, Keele 1994
The Pottery Gazette, 1953

THE DESIGNS OF KATHIE WINKLE
BY PETER LEATH

In September 1996, my wife, Sally, came home from a local car-boot sale with a tea plate which was decorated with a geometric design. On the back of the plate was the backstamp:

IRONSTONE
BROADHURST
STAFFORDSHIRE
ENGLAND
A Winkle
Kathie · DESIGN
HANDPAINTED
UNDERGLAZE
COLOUR IS DETERGENT
AND DISHWASHER PROOF
COMPASS

Sally spent most of the following day peering through catalogues and reference books looking for the name Kathie Winkle, which she was sure she had recently seen. She eventually found a coloured photograph of the plate in the 1996/7 edition of *Millers Collectables*. Thus began her search in car-boot sales, auction rooms and charity shops for more examples of Kathie Winkle china and we referred to these expeditions as 'going Winkling'.

Sometime later, I made enquiries about her in the Potteries area, and received a four-page information sheet from the Stoke-on-Trent Museum which contained a resumé of the work of Kathie Winkle. I then contacted a Stoke-on-Trent newspaper, *The Sentinel*, who thought that my quest to find out more about the designer would make an interesting article, which they duly published. As a result, I heard from Mr Eddie Orme who, as an ex-production manager for the Churchill Group, had known and worked with Kathie for many years. He told me that she was still alive, and he advised me to buy *Churchill China: British Potters Since 1795*, by Rodney Hampson, which had references to Kathie Winkle and the firm of Broadhurst & Sons. Later, I received a phone call from Kathie herself,

Outside the Broadhurst Factory, Fenton, c1960. From left to right: Peggy Kelsall, paintress; Kathie Winkle, designer; Dorothy Frost, hand-stamper; Frances Bourne, paintress.

during which I hinted, rather hesitantly, that I would like to compile a book for collectors. To my surprise, she thought this a good idea and offered me her help, and for this I will be eternally grateful.

Records and personal accounts show that at least 122 Kathie Winkle designs were put into production, many of which have been found in strange locations. Last year we went to a table-top sale in a small village hall in the Isle of Wight. I spotted a Kathie Winkle plate on a radiator. 'Oh, it's not for sale', I was told, 'it's part of the hall's china.' 'Is there more of it?', I asked. 'Lots', was the reply. Eventually, the woman in charge arrived and I managed to buy thirty-two cups, saucers and plates, including those I had retrieved from the washing-up bowl. Such is the fun of collecting! We have a small army of friends who, from their travels not only in this country but Europe, Canada and America, bring us back Kathie Winkle china which it is still possible, for a very modest outlay, to buy and collect.

Her designs are now being appreciated and collected. Marketed as mass-produced tableware, with rubber stamp printing pertinent to the period, it will find its place in the history of twentieth-century design, as will the remarkable design talent of this untrained artist.

When wartime restrictions were lifted on the home sales of decorated china there was a demand for bright and colourful kitchen ware. The availability of new materials allowed designers to create new structural shapes and designs, with plastics and laminates being widely used. These modern ideas extended into china, and firms such as T.G. Green, Midwinter and Broadhurst responded by producing startling new shapes and pattern designs.

After working at Broadhurst's for some time as a paintress, Kathie Winkle was asked if she could draw, and she said she could, '...a little'. In 1958 she began to design patterns and very soon became the in-house designer, responsible for all the Broadhurst patterns, with her very unusual geometric style. Broadhurst's was a forward-looking and innovative firm and Kathie's designs were a clear departure from the pretty floral motifs, so popular in the past. Their gamble paid off. Kathie Winkle became a household name and her 'designer-china' a best seller and, with the continued success and popularity of her designs, the firm prospered.

Kathie was a prolific designer but she says that a few of the designs bearing her backstamp were not her brainchild. She also ruefully admits that she cannot remember precisely how many were put into production with her backstamp, as many were small, special orders, which were required very quickly. So quickly in fact, that some did not have a pattern name, or even a backstamp, but just a number on the back. Kathie recalls that many designs were drawn up and designed very quickly for mail order firms such as Littlewood and Grattons, Great Universal Stores, and local retail shops and hardware stores, and were considered to be 'cheap and cheerful' tableware and not valued like their best china. Since we began collecting, Sally and I have become attuned to Kathie's style and can recognise one of her designs even if we have never seen it before.

Introduced in 1958, her first design was *Pedro*, although her name was not on the backstamp. Designs were applied by machine using rubber stamps, usually in black, which was hand-coloured by the team of paintresses. This process was called 'stamp and fill' and nearly all of Kathie's designs were produced by this technique. In the early days, Broadhurst's produced patterns such as *Maytime* (early 1950s) which had as many as five colours. During Kathie's years as a designer, to keep costs down in a competitive market, most of her designs contained no more than two or three colours, and some were single-coloured but, such was the quality of her work, this did not lessen her popularity with the public.

Concord, a striking geometric design, was not designed by Kathie. The drawing was purchased by Stephen Roper, then sales director, from Bennetts who supplied rubber stamps to the factory. He thought the design had great potential and from this came the idea of *Rushstone,* the brainchild of Reg Chilton, and drawn up for production by Kathie. The simplicity of this design with its bold, strong colours, was the very essence of this pattern.

During the 1950s and 1960s, many designs were sold in Canada and the buyers did not believe that the designer could genuinely be called 'Kathie Winkle'. So, Broadhurst brought out a backstamp with her signature, used on all her designs until 1978, when her patterns were slowly phased out. In 1984 Broadhurst was renamed Churchill Tableware and in 1992, Churchill China plc. The company was floated on the Stock Exchange in 1994.

The product range of items available in each design is illustrated on page 31, but, as collectors realise, there are certain items which are difficult to find. Tea and coffee pots are the rarest, as many were exported to Canada, America, and South Africa. Demand for them in this country was limited as the general public made do with their traditional large teapots. Other rare items in the Broadhurst range include covered vegetable dishes, gravy boats and stands, covered sugar bowls, small coffee cups and saucers, egg cups, salt and pepper pots, milk jugs and, rarest of all, two-tiered cake-stands. Some of the items in our own collection have travelled considerable distances in their short lifetime – we have pieces that were originally exported to the west coasts of Canada and America in the 1950s and 1960s, were used for thirty or forty years, and then brought back to the United Kingdom.

When compiling this book, I attempted to produce some finished 'camera-ready' artwork for a Kathie Winkle design and chose *Rushstone.* The rough outline was originally drawn by Reg Chilton but was later refined and redrawn by Kathie. As such a short time was allowed to produce samples of *Rushstone* it was impossible to produce rubber stamps, so Kathie hand-painted the whole pattern onto a set of pottery. The design was then approved by the customer, went into general production and proved to be one of the most popular patterns ever, selling in vast quantities throughout the world. This pattern is one of my favourites as it embodies the essence of a Kathie Winkle design, with a geometric pattern of squares (each taking up an eighteenth part of 360 degrees), some containing the 'bulls-eye' circle motif; the pattern is then filled in with only two colours.

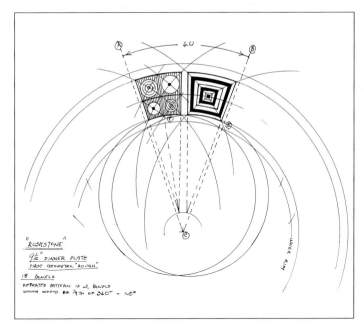

Peter Leath's technical drawing of Kathie Winkle's *Rushstone* design.

However, though *Rushstone* initially appeared to be quite a simple design, reproducing the artwork proved a most difficult task. I realised that I would have to treat it as a technical or geometric drawing as all the squares and circles had to be drawn with a ruler and compass, and quickly appreciated how much skill was involved in producing Kathie's finished artwork. In addition, I had the completed plate to work from, while she only had a rough sketch. As there were no cameras capable of reducing or enlarging the design for each article, she had to redraw the pattern each time. This had to be drawn with perfect squares and circles for the upright pattern on the hollow-ware. No mean task as can be seen by my preparatory drawing of a dinner plate pattern above. Most of Kathie's geometric designs posed similar problems for producing finished artwork for rubber stamps.

In the 1960s and 1970s the British began to travel to exotic locations for their holidays – exciting and sun-warmed places such as Acapulco, Barbados, Monte Carlo, San Tropez, Corfu, Palermo, and Palma. Designs were descriptive of these new holiday locations and none more so than *Barbados* with its tropical fruits and zig-zag patterning of the local clothing. The names of designs were also indicative of their time. *Bamboo* suggested the Far East; *Calypso,* the palm-fringed white beaches of the West Indies; *Mardis Gras,* the carnival time in South America; *Mexico,* designed for the 1970 Olympic Games; *Safari* with its border of Zulu assegai spears, interspersed with flashes of hot yellow and orange. Whether the names were given to Kathie's designs or *she* designed the patterns to match the names is a matter for conjecture, but the Broadhurst decision makers certainly worked closely with their designer. There was a highly competitive market in the industry post-1950s and Broadhurst's management recognised the need for innovative ideas and practices in order to survive.

James Broadhurst's factory staff in 1974.

POSTSCRIPT

Broadhurst's marketed numerous rubber-stamped tableware patterns in the post-war period. Some of these remained popular for many years and so were frequently reissued. From 1964, the Kathie Winkle backstamp became the official registered trademark for Broadhurst's china. Consequently, some of the pre-Kathie Winkle patterns bore the Kathie Winkle backstamp when they were later reissued. For example, *Petula*, first produced in 1955 and not designed by Kathie, when later reissued post-1964, carried her backstamp. There are many earlier pieces which *are* Kathie's designs but do not have her backstamp because the previous Broadhurst backstamps were still in use. Another anomaly is the colour schemes: *Mexico*, for example, was produced in several colourways but retained the same design name. This was usually due to a private order requiring 'exclusivity'. However, this did not always apply as some identical designs with different colourways were given separate names, e.g. *Alicante* and *Autumn Glen*, (see page 26). A number of Kathie's designs were also produced on the Sandstone Matt Glaze range (see Pattern Index).

The same pattern design can also be found on both of the main body shapes, i.e. the early *Tudor* shape with its curved tulip-shape and the later *Delta* shape with its straight sides. The latter was introduced in the early 1960s by the modeller, Stan Edge. There are some fifteen and more designs which are unavailable to us for photography –

another seven or so have only recently come to light and, again, no samples of these have been found. Several of the patterns referred to in this book are not Kathie Winkle's original ideas, but all the finished artwork was by her.

Kathie Winkle and Rod Devall, personnel manager, on her retirement in 1992.

Top and above, advertising for the American market.

Advertisement for Eatons of Canada.

PROMOTIONAL LEAFLETS

A selection of promotional leaflets.

Far left top and bottom, Broadhurst presentation packs.

Above, *Calypso* design on enamelled ovenware.

Left, *Calypso* design on a rare teapot.

Below, *Calypso* design on tableware and mugs.

ROULETTE

A new geometric design in a gay colour scheme with instant eye-appeal, this modern pattern is already proving its popularity, particularly in the mail order and store outlets, both home and overseas.

Various promotional leaflets including, above, *Rushstone* advertised on a Plumrose tin.

THE DESIGNS

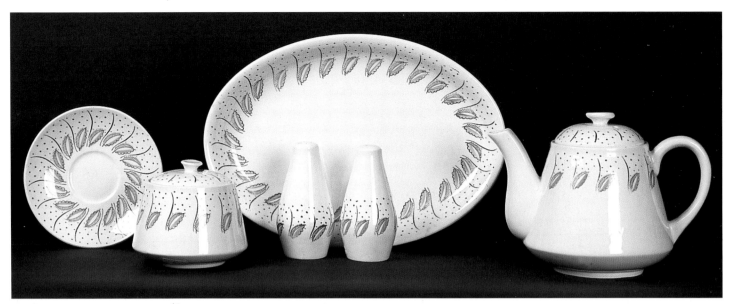

Petula

Pedro and *Bamboo*.

Albany

Autumn

Left to right, *Jamboree, Rosetta, Radiance* and *Olympus*, 1962.

Left to right, *Ascot,
Mikado* and *Majorca.*

Left to right, *Safari* and *Newlyn.*

Left to right, *Harvest A, Harvest B, Apollo* and *Edelweiss.*

Left to right, *Viscount* and *Harebell*.

Left to right, *Calypso*, *1506*, *1510* and *1511*.

Rushstone

Concord in two colourways.

Left to right, *Orchard*, *Paisley*, *Pomella* and *Wheat Rose*.

Left ro right, *Regatta*, *Monte Carlo*, *Sentinel*, *Hyde Park* and *Tarragona*.

Left to right, *Bridgewood*, *Barbados* and *Capri*.

Left to right, *Solar*, *Kontiki* and *Palermo*.

Left to right, *Michelle* and *Seattle*.

Left to right,
Corfu and
Mardi Gras.

Left to right,
Barbecue and
Compass.

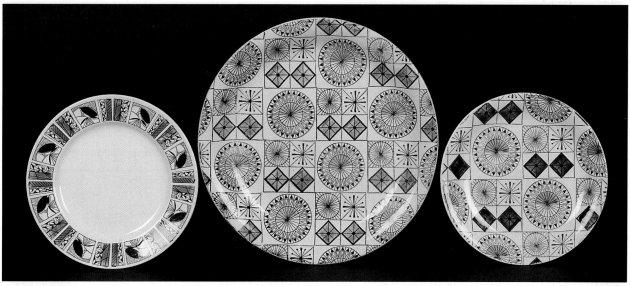

Left to right,
*Lagoon,
Mandalay, San
Tropez* and
Corinth.

Above: left to right, *Arizona*, *Acapulco*, *Venice* and *Woodland*.

Right: left to right, *Tenerife*, *Moselle* and *Geneva*.

Left to right, *Electra*, *Rebecca* and *Palma Nova*.

Leftto right,
Versailles and
Renaissance.

Left to right,
Eclipse and
Seville.

Mexico

23

Left to right, *Indian Tree* and *Manderley*.

Left to right, *Zodiac*, *Moorland* and *Sombrero*.

Left to right, *Roulette*, *Harrow 4* and *Carousel*.

Left to right, *Kimberley* and *October*.

Left to right, *Fortuna*, *Ashington*, *Silver Dawn* and *Seychelles*.

Left to right, *Wayfarer*, *Grosvenor* and *Country Lane*.

Left to right, *Alicante* and *Autumn Glen*.

Left to right, *Lemon Grove*, *Romany* and *Tashkent*.

Left to right, *Olympus 1964*, and *Agincourt*.

Left to right, *Medina*, *Vanity Fair* and *Wild Flowers*.

Alpine

Cordoba

Symphony

San Marino

Muscouri

Hillside

Gaiety

Snowdon

Morning Glory

Tahiti

Elba

Bouquet

Alton

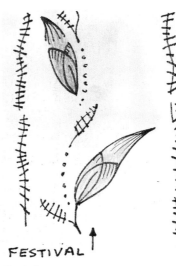

Festival

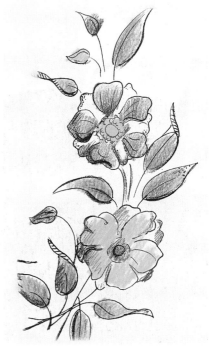

Carmen

DESIGNS TAKEN DIRECTLY
FROM BENNETT'S RUBBER STAMPS

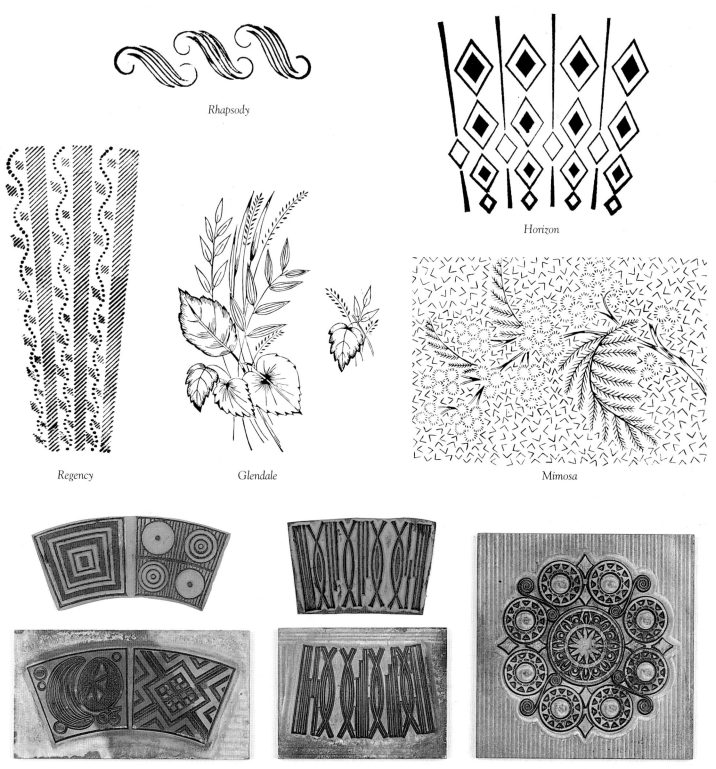

Rhapsody

Horizon

Regency

Glendale

Mimosa

Bennett's rubber stamps and the brass master plates for Kathie Winkle designs.

PATTERN INDEX

KEY TO ABBREVIATIONS:

KW: designs and artwork by Kathie Winkle

AWO: artwork only by Kathie Winkle

BSO: Kathie Winkle backstamp only

S: Sandstone matt glaze range

NI: not illustrated

SHAPE GUIDE

TUDOR

DELTA

'Tudor' teapot

'Kofti' pot

Teaplate 6¾ins

Plate 8ins

Plate 9ins

Plate 9½ins

Oatmeal 6ins

Coupe soup 8ins

Fruit 5ins

Open scollop 9ins

Salt and pepper

Gravy boat and stand

Cheese dish and cover

Oval dish 12ins

Bread and butter plate 9ins

Covered sugar

Open sugar

'Tudor' teacup

Covered vegetable dish

Coffee pot

Teapot

Cream jug

Teacup and saucer 7½oz

Coffe cup and saucer 6½oz

Egg cup

Mug

BACKSTAMPS

There were many variations on Broadhurst's backstamps. The main ones are shown below.

JAS. BROADHURST & SONS LTD. ENGLAND

From 1957

Above, above right and right: variations on the Broadhurst backstamp pre-1964.

"Broadhurst" ENGLAND HAND PAINTED UNDERGLAZE FAST COLOUR CARMEN

From 1961

STAFFORDSHIRE ENGLAND EST. SINCE 1847 Broadhurst HANDPAINTED UNDERGLAZE COLOUR IS DETERGENT AND DISHWASHER PROOF VISCOUNT

From 1961

IRONSTONE BROADHURST STAFFORDSHIRE ENGLAND A Kathie Winkle DESIGN HANDPAINTED UNDERGLAZE COLOUR IS DETERGENT AND DISHWASHER PROOF MEXICO

From 1964 The official Kathie Winkle registered trademark.

BROADHURST ENGLAND IRONSTONE Riviera Shape A Kathie Winkle DESIGN HANDPAINTED UNDERGLAZE COLOUR IS DETERGENT AND DISHWASHER PROOF CORFU

c1968

BROADHURST STAFFORDSHIRE ENGLAND IRONSTONE INDIAN TREE HANDPAINTED UNDERGLAZE COLOUR IS DETERGENT AND DISHWASHER PROOF

Sandstone BROADHURST STAFFORDSHIRE ENGLAND COLOUR HANDPAINTED UNDERGLAZE MUSCOURI

From 1972-75

Above left, adaptation of backstamp incorporating *Riviera* shape.
Above, Sandstone range backstamp.
Left, c1971. Example of backstamp for a private order.

BROADHURST & SONS CHRONOLOGY

1847 James Broadhurst I joined a partnership making 185 James Broadhurst I joined a partnership making earthenware at Green Dock Works, Longton, Stoke-on-Trent.

1853 James Broadhurst I joined an earthenware partnership at Crown Works, Longton, and left the Green Dock business.

1854 James Broadhurst I became sole proprietor of the Crown Works business.

1856 James Broadhurst I took his sons into partnership.

1858 James Broadhurst I died.

1863 James Broadhurst II became sole proprietor.

1870 James Broadhurst II moved his business to a new factory, Portland Pottery, Fenton, Stoke-on-Trent, making earthenware.

1876 James Broadhurst purchased Portland Pottery from John Aynsley.

1894 James Broadhurst II took his sons into partnership.

1897 James Broadhurst II died.

1913 Edward Roper and Llewellyn Meredith started in partnership at Garfield Works, Longton, manufacturing earthenware.

1922 James Broadhurst III formed a limited company, James Broadhurst & Sons Ltd., with himself and Edward Roper as directors. Roper and Meredith's partnership was dissolved.

1928 Edward Roper's son, Peter, joined the firm.

1929 James Broadhurst III died.

1933 James Broadhurst & Sons Ltd., bought the factory from the Broadhurst family.

1939 The company was re-formed as James Broadhurst & Sons (1939) Ltd.

1941 The factory was closed for the duration of the war. Edward Roper died, and Peter Roper joined the R.A.F.

1945 Peter Roper reopened the works, and commenced extensive modernisation, resumed making earthenware.

1950 Kathy Winkle joined the firm as a paintress.

1957 Kathie Winkle started as a designer.

1958 Peter Roper's eldest son, Michael, joined the firm. Kathie Winkle created *Pedro*, her first design.

1959 The firm reverted to the original name of James Broadhurst & Sons Ltd.

1960 Peter Roper's second son, Stephen, joined the firm.

1965 James Broadhurst bought Sampson Bridgwood & Sons Ltd., Anchor Works, Longton, hotelware manufacturers. (See below.)

1973 Peter Roper's third son, Andrew, joined the firm.

1974 Packing and warehouse space outside the two works was utilised at Montrose Works, Fenton and Sutherland Road, Longton.

1974 The Crown Clarence Works, King Street, Longton, was bought and Churchill China Ltd., (renamed Crown Clarence Ltd., in 1992) was formed to produce mugs.

1978 Kathie Winkle retired as a designer and became a quality-control manageress.

1979 James Broadhurst & Sons Ltd., bought a large modern factory, Sandyford Works, Tunstall, to provide warehousing for the group, and later to become a production unit. Wessex Ceramics Ltd., was formed to import china, glass, cutlery etc.

1981 The Portland Pottery, Fenton, was closed and production moved to Sandyford.

1984 Broadhurst's was renamed Churchill Tableware and Bridgwood's was renamed Churchill Hotelware. (The Churchill name had already been in use within the group for Churchill China since 1975 and for general publicity. The subsidiary companies were Churchill China, Stratford Bone China, W. Moorcroft, Wessex Ceramics and Staffordshire Crystal.)

1985 The British Anchor Pottery building at Longton was bought for warehousing and storage.

1989 The group was reorganised into three divisions: tableware, hotelware and mugs. Peter Roper became president and Peter Siddall became chairman.

1991 Peter Roper died, aged seventy-nine.

1991 The group purchased the Alexander Works at Cobridge. (See below.)

1992 Kathy Winkle's retirement.

1992 The group was renamed Churchill China plc.

1994 The group bought Crownford China, Longton.

1994 Floated on the Stock Exchange.